TANKS

MICHAEL GREEN

with James D. Brown and Christophe Vallier

ZENITH PRESS

ACKNOWLEDGMENTS

In addition to those mentioned in the photo credits of this book, special thanks are due to the very helpful staffs of the U.S. Army's Patton Museum of Cavalry and Armor, Fort Knox, Kentucky; the Tank Museum, Bovington, England; and the history office of the TACOM. Individuals who made an extra effort in assisting the authors but do not appear in the text or photo caption credits include Jacques Littlefield, Randy Talbot, James Warford, Dean and Nancy Kleffman, and David Fletcher.

First published in 2008 by Zenith Press, an imprint of MBI Publishing Company, 400 1st Avenue North, Suite 300, Minneapolis, MN 55401 USA.

Zenith Press titles are also available at discounts in bulk quantity for industrial or sales-promotional use. For details write to Special Sales Manager at MBI Publishing Company, 400 1st Avenue North, Suite 300, Minneapolis, MN 55401 USA.

To find out more about our books, join us online at www.zenithpress.com.

Library of Congress Cataloging-in-Publication Data

Green, Michael, 1952-
  Tanks / Michael Green, James D. Brown, and Christophe Vallier.
    p. cm.
  ISBN 978-0-7603-3351-8 (pbk. : alk. paper) 1. Tanks (Military science) I. Brown, James D. II. Vallier, Christophe. III. Title.
UG446.5.G6938 2008
623.7'4752--dc22

                        2007048147

Designer: Danielle Carnito

Printed in China

ON THE FRONT COVER:
The 120mm-main-gun-armed M103 heavy tank was to support the U.S. Army's medium tanks in battle by destroying Soviet Army heavy tanks, such as the IS-III Stalin armed with a 122mm main gun. *TACOM Historical Office*

ON THE FRONTISPIECE:
Posed at the edge of a wooded area is a former Belgian Army Leopard I tank that now belongs to a private collector. The Belgian Army acquired 334 units of the tank from its German builder beginning in 1968. *Christophe Vallier*

ON THE TITLE PAGE:
About 10,000 units of the T-72 main battle tank series remain in the inventory of the Russian Federation Army. Built under license in five other countries besides Russia, the T-72 serves in at least 30 armies. *Tank Museum, Bovington*

ABOUT THE AUTHORS:
Michael Green is a freelance writer, researcher, and photographer who specializes in military, transportation, and law enforcement subjects, with more than eighty books to his credit. In addition, he has written numerous articles for a variety of national and international military-related magazines.

James D. Brown served twenty years in the U.S. Army as an armor officer, with secondary specialty in research and development. His active duty service includes a four-year tour as an assistant professor of engineering at the United States Military Academy, where he taught combat vehicle design and automotive engineering.

Christophe Vallier is a freelance photographer who specializes in military subjects.

Contents

Introduction

Introduction

A tank is a military vehicle that provides mobile, armor-protected firepower in the direct-fire role for a ground combat formation. That is a description, not a prescription. No central authority meets to pronounce judgment on which vehicles are tanks and which are not. Each tank producer evaluates the needs of his present or intended future force, the tactics and terrain in which the tank will see action, his ability to produce and maintain the tank, and not least importantly, his ability to afford the tank fleet he has in mind.

The practical expression of the tank is younger than that of the airplane. Considering the broad diversity of intentions and capabilities among nations, it is astonishing that the short evolutionary process, begun less than a century ago, has resulted in a nearly universal design expression among the mainstream tanks of the world. Many a layman, observing the most common layout of a rear-engine tracked vehicle with a central gun turret and a forward-mounted driver's station, would be hard pressed to point out the differences among models.

This book illustrates the evolutionary process that occurred in the major tank-producing nations of the world. That process is much too complex to be conveyed in a single volume, but it is our intention to suggest the design threads that ran both along the timeline of each nation and across each respective nation as it assimilated not only its own experience, but learned from both allies and adversaries. The story of the development of the modern tank is not a mere timeline, but a rich tapestry in which each design, from the earliest days right up to the most modern production, is influenced by the international history of its predecessors.

Most of the British tanks that saw combat in World War I had the all-around tracks as seen here on this Mark V heavy tank, intended to help them cross wide trenches. *Tank Museum, Bovington*

The following few paragraphs on tank design provide a rubric against which the individual entries maybe evaluated. They enable the reader to pick out the differences that distinguish the various models and ultimately recognize the national philosophies and characteristics that characterize each nation's tanks.

An ideal tank would have mobility, protection, and firepower superior to any potential adversary. Practically, however, these three principal design attributes are often at odds in the design. The smallest, lightest vehicle possible maximizes mobility, while armor protection implies claims against volume or weight (or both). Firepower implies the largest, heaviest weapon with the most potent ammunition brought to the battlefield. The determination of a successful design comes not only from how well each of the attributes is embodied in the vehicle, but by how little the demands of each is compromised by the demands of the other two. The overarching attributes of reliability, maintainability, and affordability must be considered concurrently in the

Some of the tanks that saw service during World War II had large cannons mounted in their front hulls and smaller turret-mounted cannons. The U.S. Army M3 series medium tank is an example of that. *National Archives*

design process. However, the focus of a tank's design must be on how to ensure that it can get to where it needs to go, that it survives long enough to influence the battle, and that it brings enough firepower to make the effort worthwhile.

Mobility of a tank must satisfy its user's needs in both the strategic sense and the tactical sense. Strategic mobility addresses the requirement to move the tank to wherever in the world the need arises. The movement can be made under the tank's own power, but is more often dependent on other modes of transportation, such as land, sea, or air transports. Considerations of overall dimensions, total weight, and ground pressure dominate the strategic mobility question, and as soon as the characteristics of those transportation modes are understood, they become guidelines from which the designer may stray only at his peril. Tactical mobility is more complex because the terrains and environmental conditions the tank will operate in may not be foreseen during the design phase or may be so generalized as to be of little practical use to the designer.

The three subject areas that broadly encompass the tactical mobility of a tank are ground pressure, power-to-weight ratio, and suspension. The obvious consideration of ground pressure is that a vehicle not break through soft soils and become mired. However, the ability to transmit propulsive forces evenly over as large an area as possible is the real key to understanding ground pressure.

In the tanks of almost all nations, the means of minimizing ground pressure has evolved into a solution of full tracks with between five and seven road-wheel stations on each side. This is not because some rulebook says tanks must have tracks, but because tracks spread the vehicle weight and track loads over a larger area than wheels would alone. In most designs, fewer than five road wheels results in undesirable load concentrations into the soil, and more than seven requires road-wheel diameter to be reduced, which results in higher rolling resistance.

Power-to-weight ratio is the principal measure of how well a tank can accelerate and how well it can maintain its speed up a hill. Contrary to Hollywood's depiction of tanks as lumbering behemoths whose cumbersome approach builds dramatic tension and gives the actors more time for dialogue, modern tanks are both fast and agile vehicles whose ability to traverse terrain at high speeds will astonish the inexperienced. A formidable characteristic of the tank, its so-called "shock action," is a consequence not only of its mind-numbing firepower, but its ability to interject itself upon the scene before its opponent can consider his own course of action. Speed and agility contribute to survivability of the tank not only by making it a more difficult target, but by cutting inside its adversary's decision cycle by reducing the time he has to decide what to do next.

Early tank designs often used gasoline engines because they were the lightest, most

Taking part in a public display is an M4 Sherman medium tank belonging to the Patton Museum of Cavalry and Armor. Almost 50,000 rolled out of American factories during World War II. *Chu Hsu*

efficient engines of the day. As internal combustion technology evolved, diesel engines and gas turbines became practical. Tank designs using gas turbines for all or part of their power have been fielded by the United States, Russia, and Sweden and have been experimented with by other nations. Turbines are much smaller and lighter than diesels of corresponding power, but their stringent air supply demands (in both quantity and cleanliness of combustion air) somewhat offset their desirability. Hybrid electric propulsion is attractive, not only from a noise and smoke reduction aspect, but because availability of a powerful electric source aboard the tank opens the possibility of electrically powered weapons. However, the weight and volume of current electric propulsion systems, as well as their cost, leaves diesels or gas turbines as the engines of choice in the near future.

Suspension design must allow the vehicle to encounter surface irregularities as the vehicle traverses the ground. A good suspension not only protects the crew from bone-jarring impacts, but provides a stable weapon platform and allows the tractive effort of the powertrain to be continuously transmitted into the ground. This implies not only large excursions of suspension travel, but also efficient damping to absorb energy induced into the vehicle from the ground. Most modern tank suspensions use transverse torsion bars, with one end anchored to the opposite side of the hull, leading across the hull to a trailing arm suspension unit. Hydro-pneumatic units are also available and offer potential reduction in hull height because the units do not have space claims in the hull bottom. However, hydro-pneumatic suspensions are costly to acquire and maintain, and their use has thus far been limited to a few specialized vehicles and technology demonstrators.

Although some wheeled vehicles present impressive capabilities on roads or unchallenging terrains, their ability to traverse the toughest terrains at tactically significant speeds (if at all), to absorb punishing terrain-induced loads, and to tolerate and survive battle damage means that mainstream tank design will continue to incorporate full-tracked suspensions with diesel or turbine engines in the foreseeable future.

Armor protection has historically consisted of solid plates or spaced arrays of steel armor. Modern designs are beginning to exploit the capabilities of composite armors, in which protection comes not only from the strength of the armor material but by the geometry and composition of its interior design. Unfortunately, the details of such advanced designs are jealously guarded and highly classified information. It must suffice to say that the armor protection of modern vehicles far exceeds that which may be deduced from exterior inspection and comparison to all-steel designs. That is to say, the nearly 2-foot-thick frontal armor apparent from photos of a U.S. Abrams or British Challenger tank is far superior to a mere 2-foot-thick slab of the best steel armor. The cutting-edge technology of protection is in active protection systems, which reach out to destroy incoming projectiles before they hit the tank. The most advanced system has already demonstrated the ability to knock down any available tank-fired ammunition, rocket-propelled grenade (RPG) launchers, antitank guided missiles (ATGM), mortars, and artillery while on the move. Fielding of such a system is imminent in several armies.

Tank firepower is almost universally expressed in high-velocity cannons capable of firing a variety of kinetic energy and high-explosive projectiles. Although all the major tank-producing nations have at one time or another fielded or experimented

The U.S. Army answer to the Soviet Army's heavy tanks fielded during the Cold War (1949–1991) was the M103 heavy tank armed with a very long and powerful 120mm main gun. *Patton Museum of Cavalry and Armor*

with guided projectiles, the rate of fire of tank-fired guided missiles, along with their practical limitation as high-explosive-only warheads, has not led to their broad adoption. The accuracy of modern tank guns, along with sophisticated fire control and target acquisition suites, means that tanks are now capable of finding and hitting virtually any target they can see. Indeed, the accuracy of modern tank guns is superior to the best sniper rifles at ranges beyond 1,500 meters, and first-round hits are the norm. Although electromagnetic guns have been in development for many years, it appears that relatively conventional cannons will be the gold standard of tank armament for years to come.

As you read through this book, we invite you to connect the dots and draw your own conclusions about the various tank designs. Look for the bloodlines of each design, and you will see how tank design has evolved through the decades. Even the most surprising tank concepts are expressions of lessons learned, adversaries measured up, and the designers' best efforts to provide the best mobility, armor protection, and firepower for their ground forces.

(below) The Japanese Army Type 74 main battle tank began production in 1974. Armed with a British-designed 105mm main gun, it featured well-sloped turret and hull armor. *Tank Museum, Bovington*

(opposite page, top) American Marines operate a Russian-designed T-72 main battle tank during a peacetime training exercise. Using foreign-built tanks in training exercises allow Marines to become conversant with the tanks of possible future opponents. *Defense Visual Information Center*

(opposite page, bottom) The West German Army depended on the superiority of the Leopard II main battle tank, armed with a powerful and extremely accurate 120mm main gun, throughout the 1980s to defend its borders. *Krauss-Maffei*

A vehicle commander on a U.S. Army M60A3 tank looks through his laser rangefinder while his gunner, directly below and in front of him, looks through his primary sight. *Defense Visual Information Center*

During the latter half of the 1980s, the cutting edge of British Army tank technology came to be the Challenger I main tank, armed with a 120mm main gun. Its replacement was the Challenger II. *Tank Museum, Bovington*

(opposite page, bottom) The American military's Cold War counterpart to the West German Army's Leopard II tank was the Abrams main battle tank originally armed with a 105mm main gun and later a 120mm main gun, as seen here. *Department of Defense*

British Tanks

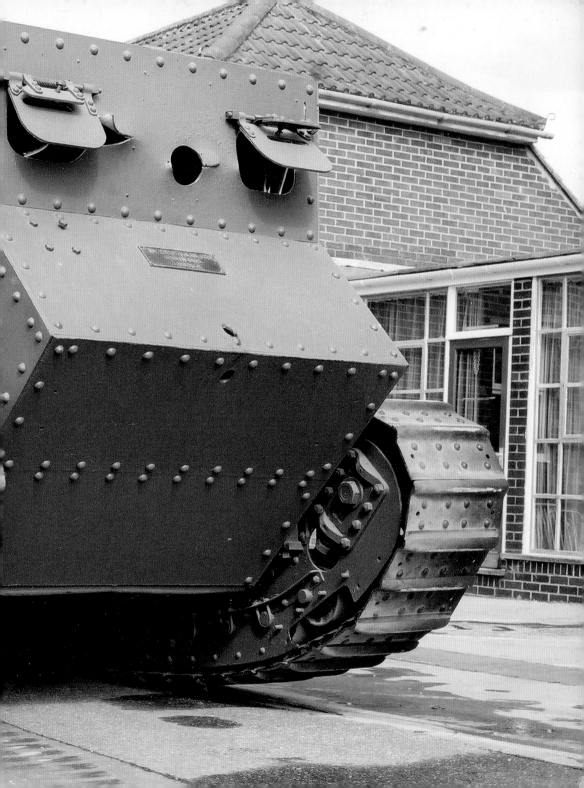

British Tanks

The British military saw the tank as an answer to the trench-locked stalemate that developed in Western Europe, during the early stages of World War I. Once that need was recognized, some basic requirements appeared in June 1915 for an armored tracked vehicle. In quick order appeared a couple of experimental prototypes, the first being a box-like vehicle nicknamed Little Willie and a second vehicle with a rhomboidal shape, nicknamed Mother. From the design of Mother evolved the roughly 30-ton Mark I turretless heavy tank series that first entered action against the German Army in September 1916. The British Army would field progressively improved versions of the Mark I during the remainder of World War I.

Following World War I, some farsighted individuals in the British Army championed the continued development of the tank. Sadly, the senior British Army hierarchy failed to embrace the tank. This indifference to the continued development of the tank came back to haunt the British Army when the outbreak of World War II, in September 1939, found their tank inventory consisted of an assortment of unremarkable and indifferently designed tanks, which proved unreliable in the field and inferior to their German counterparts.

It was not until the closing stages of World War II in mid-1945, that the British Army managed to field a tank that stood a chance of successfully engaging late-war German tanks. That tank was named the Centurion and unfortunately arrived too late to see action before the surrender of Nazi Germany, in May 1945.

To keep the Centurion up to date when compared with newer generations of tanks designed and built after World War II, the

The vehicle pictured was nicknamed Little Willie and was the direct forerunner of all British tanks. Built in September 1915, Little Willie never saw combat and was used only for testing track and steering designs. *Tank Museum, Bovington*

British Army and other users of the tank took to upgrading every aspect of its design. This continuous process of modification allowed the Centurion to serve in a frontline combat role through the early 1990s, until superseded in most armies by more modern tanks.

In support of the Centurion tank in the mid-1950s, the British Army had introduced into service the roughly 73-ton Conqueror heavy tank armed with a huge 120mm main gun. Its job was to deal with Russian heavy tanks like the IS-3 Stalin tank, at longer ranges than the 50-ton Centurion could. Sadly, the Conqueror suffered from a number of design problems that it never overcame and passed from use in 1966. This was the same year the Centurion replacement, known as the Chieftain, first appeared in service with the British Army.

While the Chieftain also featured a 120mm main gun, like the Conqueror, the version of the main gun on the Chieftain

MARK I HEAVY TANK	
Length:	32 feet 6 inches
Width:	13 feet 9 inches
Height:	8 feet
Approximate Weight:	34 tons
Crew:	8
Armament:	two 57mm cannons and four to six machine guns

The Mark I heavy tank first saw combat with the British Army in September 1916, against the German Army in France. The wooden wheels attached to the rear of the tank aided in steering the vehicle. *Tank Museum, Bovington*

was a new design that was both lighter and more effective in every respect than the gun of the same caliber on the Conqueror. While the Chieftain's firepower and armor protection set new standards for excellence in tank design when introduced into service, it had serious mobility problems related to its unreliable diesel engine.

The replacement for the Chieftain in British Army proved to be the Challenger, which first appeared in service in 1983. While using the same main gun as the Chieftain, the armor protection on the Challenger was of the latest design and far superior to that on the Chieftain. Problems with the fire-control system on the original Challenger led to fielding in the early 1990s of an upgraded version of the tank called the Challenger 2, which is now the mainstay of the British Army ground forces.

Differing in some minor design details from the Mark I heavy tank was the Mark II heavy tank. This particular preserved example is equipped only with machine guns and was therefore classified as a female tank. *Tank Museum, Bovington*

On display at the U.S. Army Ordnance Museum is this Mark IV heavy tank. Like the Mark I through Mark III heavy tanks that preceded it into British Army service, it had an eight-man crew. *Michael Green*

The Mark V heavy tank was the last of the rhomboidal-shaped tanks to see combat with the British Army in World War I. The white metal semaphores on the top of the vehicle transmitted orders between tanks. *Tank Museum, Bovington*

TRACKS
Tanks carry their own portable roads, called tracks. The tank lays the tracks down in front of itself and then picks them up as it moves away. The tracks are belts made up of interlocking track links (or shoes) connected by steel pins.

In order to exploit any battlefield breakthroughs of German defensive positions during World War I by their heavy tanks, the British Army took into service the tank pictured, referred to as the Whippet medium tank. *Tank Museum, Bovington*

A replacement for the Mark I through Mark V heavy tank series was the Hornet medium tank. Of the 6,000 ordered by the British Army in October 1918, only 36 came off the production line before World War I ended in November 1918. *Patton Museum of Cavalry and Armor*

EARLY INTERNAL TANK COMMUNICATIONS
The original World War I British heavy tanks had no internal tank communication devices. A loud voice was key, and since it was possible to move around the inside of early tanks you could get sufficiently close to yell into the ear of a fellow crewman. Using hand signals was also an option, but often hard to see within the dark and often dusty confines of the vehicle.

Built in 1925, the Independent featured five separate weapon-armed revolving turrets. There was no production order for the Independent because the British Army lacked the money to buy it at the time. *Tank Museum, Bovington*

Wanting something cheaper than the Independent, the British Army acquired 130 of the Vickers medium tank, Mark II. They entered service in 1925 and were still in use when World War II started. *Tank Museum, Bovington*

VICKERS MEDIUM TANK, MARK II	
Length:	17 feet 6 inches
Width:	9 feet 2 inches
Height:	9 feet 11 inches
Approximate Weight:	15 tons
Crew:	5
Armament:	47mm cannon and three machine guns

Between 1930 and 1940, the firm of Vickers supplied the British Army a series of machine-gun-armed light tanks designated the Mark I through Mark VI. The vehicle pictured is a Mark VI and featured a three-man crew. *Tank Museum, Bovington*

In the 1930s, Vickers, the supplier of light tanks to the British Army, decided to sell versions of the same vehicles on the commercial market. Buyers of their products included the Swiss Army, which acquired the tank seen here. *Andreas Kirchhoff*

Entering British Army service in 1937 was the Cruiser tank, Mark I. It had three turrets, the largest mounting a 2-pounder (40mm) main gun and a coaxial machine gun, while the two smaller turrets had machine guns only. *Tank Museum, Bovington*

THE MEANING OF "POUNDER"
The British Army often used the approximate weight of a round fired from a gun—be it a tank gun, an antitank gun, or an artillery piece—to describe the weapon before, during, and after World War II. The U.S. Army describes their weapons by using the bore size of the weapon in millimeters (mm) or in inches, as do most armies.

The Cruiser tank, Mark IIA CS, was an up-armored version of the Cruiser tank, Mark I. Instead of a 2-pounder (40mm) main gun, it boasted a 3.7-inch, close-support howitzer. It entered British Army service in 1940. *Tank Museum, Bovington*

(opposite page, top) In 1934, the British Army decided it needed a dedicated infantry support tank. This entered into production in 1937 and was called Matilda I. The two-man tank had a single machine gun, as seen here. *Tank Museum, Bovington*

(opposite page, bottom) A replacement for the Matilda I proved to be the larger and heavier Matilda II, or just Matilda, armed with a 2-pounder (40mm) main gun and a single machine gun. Production started in 1937 and continued until 1943. *Tank Museum, Bovington*

> **DESERT CAMOUFLAGE**
> British tanks from the North Africa fighting sometimes appeared in "Mirage," or "Desert Shimmer," camouflage, which combined sky and earth colors. The theory was that a distant tank could blend in to the heat shimmer, which reflected the boundary between earth and sky.

MATILDA INFANTRY SUPPORT TANK

Length:	18 feet 5 inches
Width:	8 feet 6 inches
Height:	8 feet 3 inches
Approximate Weight:	30 tons
Crew:	4
Armament:	2-pounder (40mm) cannon and one machine gun

This photograph shows the view looking inside the restored turret of a Matilda infantry support tank from the vehicle commander's overhead hatch. Visible are both the tank commander and gunner seats. *Michael Green*

In the camouflage scheme of the British Army 1st Armored Division of 1940 is this Cruiser Mark IV armed with a 2-pounder (40mm) main gun. The tank saw combat in France and North Africa between 1940 and 1941. *Tank Museum, Bovington*

Delivered to the British Army in early 1940 was the Cruiser tank, Mark V, also referred to as the Covenanter. Plagued by a number of design faults, it saw use only as training tank in World War II. *Tank Museum, Bovington*

The Crusader III tank pictured was descended from the same line of development that resulted in the production of the Covenanter. This version mounts a 6-pounder (57mm) main gun and two machine guns. It first appeared in service in 1942. *Tank Museum, Bovington*

The Valentine III had a four-man crew and was armed with a 2-pounder (40mm) main gun and a single machine gun. The first tank in the Valentine series entered service in 1940. Production of all versions ended in 1944. *Tank Museum, Bovington*

Carried onboard gliders and dropped behind German lines in France on D-Day (June 6, 1944) was the British Army Tetrarch VII two-man light tank armed with a 2-pounder (40mm) main gun and a single machine gun. *Tank Museum, Bovington*

The Infantry tank, Mark IV—
"Churchill I"—seen here features
a 2-pounder (40mm) gun in the
revolving turret and a 3-inch
howitzer mounted in the front hull.
It first appeared in service in June
1941. *Phil Hatcher*

WHERE DID THE "CHURCHILL" IN CHURCHILL TANK COME FROM?
The British Army named the Churchill tank in honor of Sir Winston Leonard Spencer Churchill, a British politician who served as Prime Minister of Great Britain from 1940 through 1945 and led that country to victory over Nazi Germany during World War II.

As World War II progressed, the British Army continuously upgraded the main armament of the Churchill tank series. The tank pictured is the Churchill VII with a 75mm main gun. *Tank Museum, Bovington*

The crews of many British tanks, such as the Churchill VII pictured, welded extra track links to the exterior of their vehicles to provide additional protection from antitank weapons late in World War II. *Patton Museum of Cavalry and Armor*

CHURCHILL VII	
Length:	24 feet 5 inches
Width:	10 feet 8 inches
Height:	8 feet 2 inches
Approximate Weight:	45 tons
Crew:	5
Armament:	75mm cannon and two machine guns

Built too late to see action in World War II was a heavily modified version of the Churchill tank, named the Black Prince. Armed with a 17-pounder (76.2mm) main gun, only six were ever completed. *Tank Museum, Bovington*

A shortage of tanks in 1940 pushed the British Government to order a modified version of the American-designed and -built M3 series medium tank mounting a British-designed turret. It received the official nickname of General Grant. *Tank Museum, Bovington*

British tankers in North Africa climb onboard their M4 series medium tanks, nicknamed the Sherman. The British Army received its first Sherman tank in August 1942 and had more than 15,000 in service by December 1944. *Patton Museum of Cavalry and Armor*

TANK SIGHTS
A gunner in a tank traditionally aims at a target with the aid of an optical sighting instrument (telescope), which presents a magnified image of the target to his eyes. At the same time, he sees an image of a reticle, or reference mark, located inside the sighting instrument. By accurately superimposing the reticle image on the target image, the gunner can establish an accurate line of sight to the target.

The British Army mounted a 17-pounder (76.2mm) main gun in some Sherman tanks, as seen here, in order to penetrate the thick armor on late-war German tanks. They sometimes referred to it as the Firefly. *David Marian*

To increase the combat effectiveness of their American-supplied M10 tank destroyers originally armed with a 3-inch main gun, the British Army mounted a 17-pounder (76.2mm) main gun and designated them the M10C 17-pounder. *Christophe Vallier*

The Cromwell was numerically the most important British Army tank the last two years of World War II in Western Europe. The version pictured mounts a 75mm main gun. *Michael Green*

(opposite page, top) The British Army Cruiser tank, Comet—armed with a cut-down 17-pounder (76.2mm) main gun—appeared late in World War II. It was essentially an up-gunned Cromwell and served until replaced by the postwar Centurion tank. *Christophe Vallier*

(opposite page, bottom) To place as many tanks into service with the 17-pounder (76.2mm) main gun as possible, the British Army built a tank using as many Cromwell components as possible. That vehicle became the Challenger seen here. *Tank Museum, Bovington*

> **ARMOR PLACEMENT**
> Steel armor is heavy and weight restrictions on the movement of tanks means that there are limits to a vehicle's tonnage. Tank designers therefore maximize the armor effectiveness on a tank by placing the thickest armor on locations most likely struck in battle. These have historically been on the front of a tank's turret and hull.

On display at the Israeli Army Tank Museum is a post–World War II British Army Charioteer tank destroyer. It consisted of a Cromwell hull with a new turret armed with a 20-pounder (83.4mm) main gun. *Robert Manasherob*

Conceived in 1943, the first six production units of the British Army Centurion tank came off the production line in May 1945. The version pictured is the Mark III armed with a 20-pounder (83.4mm) main gun. *Tank Museum, Bovington*

CENTURION III

Length with main gun forward:	32 feet 4 inches
Width:	10 feet 10 inches
Height:	9 feet 10 inches
Approximate Weight:	57 tons
Crew:	4
Armament:	83.4mm cannon and two machine guns

Of the roughly 4,000 Centurion tanks built, more than half went to armies besides the British. The Centurion tanks pictured belong to the Indian Army and mount a 105mm main gun. *Patton Museum of Cavalry and Armor*

This late-model Centurion tank armed with a 105mm main gun sports a Swedish Army camouflage paint scheme. The large metal boxes on the front of the tank's hull and turret are explosive reactive armor (ERA) tiles. *David Marian*

THE PURPOSE OF TANK TRACKS
Tracks distribute the weight of a tank over soft ground. The heavier a tank is, the wider the tracks need to be in order to allow it to operate over soft ground. Early tank tracks in World War I had a life span of between 20 and 60 miles. Modern tank tracks can last over 3,000 miles.

(opposite page, top) As older-generation tanks become obsolete, they go on to perform other roles. The vehicle pictured is a heavily modified British Army Centurion tank configured as a target tank for infantry hand held antitank weapons. *Phil Hatcher*

(opposite page, bottom) The largest and heaviest post–World War II tank proved to be the British Army Conqueror heavy tank, armed with a 120mm main gun. It first appeared in service in 1956 and lasted until the early 1960s. *Tank Museum, Bovington*

CONQUEROR HEAVY TANK	
Length with main gun forward:	38 feet
Width:	13 feet 1 inch
Height:	11 feet
Approximate Weight:	73 tons
Crew:	4
Armament:	120mm cannon and one machine gun

Taking part in a parade is an Indian Army Vijayanta (Victory) main battle tank armed with a 105mm main gun. Designed by the British firm Vickers, the Indian Army took 2,200 into service. *Tank Museum, Bovington*

The British Army began thinking about a replacement for the Centurion tank in the early 1950s. The eventual replacement was the Chieftain tank armed with a British-designed 120mm main gun. *Tank Museum, Bovington*

(opposite page, top) Prior to the collapse of East Germany in 1989, the British Army Chieftain tanks based in West Berlin featured a camouflage paint scheme optimized for fighting in an urban city, as seen in this parade picture. *Defense Visual Information Center*

(opposite page, bottom) Classified as a reconnaissance vehicle, the Scorpion is a light tank armed with a 76mm main gun and a single machine gun. It entered British Army service in 1973 and lasted until the early 1990s. *Michael Green*

The Challenger I tank seen here was the replacement for the Chieftain tank in British Army service. Armed with the same 120mm main gun as mounted on its predecessor, it boasted improved mobility and armor protection. *Tank Museum, Bovington*

(opposite page, top) An upgraded version of the Challenger I tank appeared in British Army service in 1994 and received the designation Challenger II. The last of the 386 Challenger II tanks built entered British Army service in 2002. *Tank Museum, Bovington*

(opposite page, bottom) The Challenger II pictured has been fitted with passive armored skirts alongside its suspension system and explosive reactive armor (ERA) tiles on the front of the hull. *Tank Museum, Bovington*

CHALLENGER II

Length with main gun forward:	27 feet 4 inches
Width:	11 feet 6.5 inches
Height:	8 feet 2 inches
Approximate Weight:	69 tons
Crew:	4
Armament:	120mm gun and two machine guns

MORTIER SCHNEIDER
France
1916

75 mm
200 m/s

French Tanks

French Tanks

The idea that tanks might break the trench warfare stalemate on the Western Front during World War I had occurred to both the British and French armies at roughly the same time. While the British Army concentrated on turretless heavy tanks, such as the Mark I through V, optimized for crossing enemy trenches and assisting the infantry in the assault, the French Army's turretless, lightly armored heavy tanks, known as the Schneider and the Saint Chamond, were conceived only as mobile artillery vehicles and therefore lacked the trench-crossing ability of their British counterparts and took terrible losses from German antitank defensive measures.

While the French Army heavy tank program proved a failure in World War I, their light tank program, initiated in the summer of 1916, proved much more successful and resulted in the design and development of the innovative two-man FT-17. The new French light tank differed significantly from those tanks that came before it because it featured a weapon-armed turret that was capable of 360 degrees of traverse. Earlier turretless tank designs had their weapons firing out from the hull, with limited traverse only.

The first prototype of the FT-17 appeared in early 1917, but production delays pushed the fielding of the tank into combat until May 1917. Of the 7,820 ordered by the French Army, about half made it into service before World War I in Europe ended in November 1918. Despite the cancellation of the remainder of the FT-17 order on the conclusion of the conflict, the vehicle would remain the most important and numerous French Army tank in service until the early 1930s.

The French designed and built their first tank, the six-man Schneider, in 1916. However, it did not see combat until April 1917. Thin armor and poor off-road mobility made it a failure in service. *Christophe Vallier*

It took the Spanish Civil War, which lasted from July 1936 until April 1939 and involved the use of tanks, before the French Army decided that it needed a new generation of tanks to remain a viable force on any future battlefield with its historical foe, Germany. The French budget of 1935 allocated a substantial amount of money to the design, development, and production of a variety of new light, medium, and heavy tanks. They did not begin to reach the French Army in large numbers until early 1940. While the rush into production of new tanks resulted in some design shortcomings, such as one-man turrets, they tended to be well armed and armored compared with their German counterparts of the same time period.

Free French Army units began receiving American-supplied tanks in 1943. The post–World War II French Army continued to use American-supplied tanks and leftover German tanks until such time the French industry once again could design and build their own tanks in sufficient numbers.

The first example of these showed up in the early 1950s as the AMX-13 light tank armed with a 75mm main gun. The AMX-30 main battle tank, armed with a 105mm main, appeared in French Army service in the late 1960s.

The current French main battle tank bears the name Leclerc, in honor of a famous French Army general from World War II. Armed with a 120mm main gun fed by a 22-round automatic loader, the Leclerc can fire up to 12 rounds per minute if required. The use of an automatic loader on the tank has reduced the vehicle's crew to three men: the vehicle commander, gunner, and driver.

The vehicle commander and gunner on the Leclerc use a sophisticated computer-directed fire-control system combined with a stabilized sighting system to achieve very high first-round-hit probability. Besides having a very low silhouette and advanced forms of armor protection, the Leclerc has a self-defense system that fires off infrared and electromagnetic flares to divert incoming antitank weapons.

A Schneider heavy tank drives onto a trailer at the factory that built it for shipment to the French Army. Top speed of the 16-ton tank was just under 5 miles per hour. *Tank Museum, Bovington*

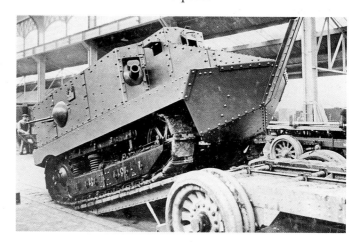

The French Army Saint Chamond heavy tank first saw combat against the German Army in May 1917. It was not a success in battle due to its inability to cross wide German trenches.
Christophe Vallier

SAINT CHAMOND TANK

Length with main gun forward:	28 feet 6 inches
Width:	8 feet 9 inches
Height:	7 feet 9 inches
Approximate Weight:	24 tons
Crew:	8
Armament:	75mm cannon and four machine guns

Pictured is an early prototype of the French Army Saint Chamond heavy tank. Top speed of the vehicle was 5 miles per hour, and power came from a four-cylinder gasoline engine that developed 90 horsepower. *Tank Museum, Bovington*

Disappointment in the design of the Schneider and Saint Chamond heavy tanks led the French Army to put its faith in the two-man Renault FT-17 light tank, which first saw combat in May 1918. *Tank Museum, Bovington*

RENAULT FT 17
France 1917

French factories built about 3,000 units of the roughly 7 1/2-ton Renault FT-17 light tank during the last two years of World War I. It would survive in French Army service through the summer of 1940. *Christophe Vallier*

THE FATHER OF FRENCH TANKS
An artillery officer, Colonel (later promoted to General) Baptiste Estienne, proved to be the man who pushed the French Army into adopting light and heavy tanks for service in World War I. While he did not invent any part of them, he was the person who conceived them.

The 77-ton Char 2C heavy tank appeared in service with the French Army the last year of World War I, but did not see combat. Upgraded in the 1930s, the Germans destroyed them in World War II. *Tank Museum, Bovington*

Armed only with a single machine gun, the Renault AMR-33 light tank reflected the cavalry branch of the French Army's interest in a light reconnaissance tank. It entered service in 1934. *Christophe Vallier*

The Hotchkiss H-39 light tank was nothing more than an up-armored version of the Hotchkiss H-35 light tank equipped with a more powerful engine. Both tanks had the 37mm main gun. *Christophe Vallier*

(opposite page, top) Renault decided in the early 1930s to develop a new light tank to meet French Army requirements. That vehicle turned out to be the three-man AMC-35 armed with either a 25mm or 47mm main gun. *Christophe Vallier*

(opposite page, bottom) Rather than accept one type of new light tank into service in the late 1930s, the French Army took several different types of light tanks into service, including the Hotchkiss H-35 seen here. *Thomas Anderson*

> **TANK LAYOUT**
> It was the French Army World War I FT-17 light tank that set the pattern for almost all tank layouts up until today. That entailed a driving compartment in the front hull of the tank, a centrally mounted fighting compartment topped by a 360-degree rotating turret carrying the vehicle's main weapon, and the engine compartment in the rear hull.

Looking almost identical to the Hotchkiss H-35 and H-39 light tank was the Renault R-35 light tank. Almost 2,000 were in service with the French Army when the German military invaded France in the summer of 1940. *Christophe Vallier*

RENAULT R-35 LIGHT TANK

Length:	13 feet 10 inches
Width:	6 feet 1 inch
Height:	7 feet 9 inches
Approximate Weight:	11 tons
Crew:	2
Armament:	37mm cannon and one machine gun

Entering French Army service in 1939 was the somewhat futuristic-looking, two-man FCM-36 light tank. Armament on the roughly 12-ton vehicle consisted of a 37mm main gun and a single machine gun. *Christophe Vallier*

The three-man Somua S-35 was the standard French Army medium tank when the Germans invaded France in the summer of 1940. The German Army thought highly enough of the tank to take it into service. *Michael Green*

A serious problem with the Somua S-35 medium tanks—and with many other French tanks—was the one-man turrets that forced the vehicle commanders to be both the gunner and loader. *Patton Museum of Cavalry and Armor*

SOMUA S-35 MEDIUM TANK	
Length:	17 feet 11 inches
Width:	6 feet 11 inches
Height:	8 feet 10 inches
Approximate Weight:	22 tons
Crew:	3
Armament:	47mm main gun and one machine gun

The water-cooled gasoline engine and transmission resided in the rear hull of the French Army Somua S-35 medium tank. In the front hull were the driver on the left and the radioman on the right. *Tank Museum, Bovington*

The best-armed tank in the French Army at the start of World War II was the four-man Char B1 bis heavy tank. It mounted a 75mm howitzer in the front hull and a 47mm gun on the turret. *Christophe Vallier*

CHAR B1 BIS HEAVY TANK
Length:	21 feet 5 inches
Width:	8 feet 11 inches
Height:	9 feet 2 inches
Approximate Weight:	35 tons
Crew:	4
Armament:	47mm gun and 75mm howitzer, plus two machine guns

FRENCH TANK DESIGN CONTRIBUTION

The French Army pioneered the use of controlled differential steering in 1926 with their Char B1 bis heavy tank. With controlled differential steering, the motion of the differential, which divided power between two output shafts, allowed a tank driver to control his vehicle with steering levers that applied brakes to one side or the other for turning his tank.

Char B1 bis heavy tanks of the French Army take part in a pre–World War II parade. Top speed of the vehicle was 17 miles per hour. Power came from a gasoline engine that generated 307 horsepower. *Patton Museum of Cavalry and Armor*

Beginning in November 1943, Free French Army units in North Africa began to receive large numbers of the diesel-powered M4A2 Sherman medium tanks. The U.S. Army preferred to use the gasoline-powered version of the Sherman tank. *Christophe Vallier*

Following World War II, the French Army fought long and hard, from 1946 until 1953, to maintain Indochina within the French sphere of influence. Much of their equipment was American-supplied, such as is this M4A1 Sherman tank. *Jim Mesko collection*

Among the many pieces of military equipment supplied to the French military during the latter part of World War II and the war in Indochina was the American four-man M5 series of light tanks. *Chun Hsu*

In late 1950, the French Army began receiving the first of over 1,200 units of the U.S. Army M24 Chaffee light tank. The four-man tank weighed about 20 tons and had a 75mm main gun. *Christophe Vallier*

The French Army continued to use various versions of the American M4 Sherman medium tank series up through the late 1950s. The Sherman tank pictured in French markings mounts a 76mm main gun. *Christophe Vallier*

Having no armament industry to speak of at the conclusion of World War II forced the French Army to use wartime German tanks, such as the Panther medium tank, through the late 1940s. *Ground Power Magazine*

The fear of a Soviet military invasion of Western Europe in the early 1950s prompted the American government to supply the French Army with a large number of M47 Patton medium tanks. *Christophe Vallier*

Not wanting to depend on foreign tanks and wishing to rebuild their own armament industry, the French Army issued a requirement in 1946 calling for a new light tank. The result was the AMX-13. *Tank Museum, Bovington*

AMX-13 Light Tank (with 75mm main gun)	
Length with main gun forward:	20 feet 10 inches
Width:	8 feet 2 inches
Height:	7 feet 7 inches
Approximate Weight:	16.5 tons
Crew:	3
Armament:	75mm cannon and one machine gun

The three-man AMX-13 light tank mounted a copy of the German Panther tank 75mm main gun. The most unusual feature of the vehicle was its oscillating turret and automatic loader. *Robert Manasherob*

OSCILLATING TURRETS
The oscillating turret offered advantages in simplified fire control, because the sights where fixed with respect to the main gun. This layout also made possible a very simple automatic loader. However, the large mass of the combined main gun and turret made it impractical to stabilize the weapon for firing on the move.

The French Army later upgraded its inventory of AMX-13 light tanks by mounting a 90mm main gun on the vehicle. A 105mm-main-gun-armed version of the tank, seen here, went to the Dutch Army. *Christophe Vallier*

The Austrian Army fielded a tracked armored vehicle of their own design with an AMX-13 turret in 1973, armed with a 105mm main gun. It received the designation SK-105 Kurassier light tank. *Tank Museum, Bovington*

During the 1956 Arab-Israeli War, the Israeli Army captured a small number of Egyptian Army Sherman tanks that featured the turret of the French AMX-13 light tank, armed with a 75mm main gun. *Robert Manasherob*

(opposite page, top) The replacement for the M47 Patton medium tank in French Army service proved to be the AMX-30 main battle tank, which mounted a 105mm main gun. *Christophe Vallier*

(opposite page, bottom) The 37-ton, four-man AMX-30 main battle tank first entered into French Army service in 1967. Top speed of the diesel-engine-powered vehicle was 40 miles per hour. *Tank Museum, Bovington*

AMX-30 MAIN BATTLE TANK

Length with main gun forward:	31 feet 1 inch
Width:	10 feet 2 inches
Height:	9 feet 4 inches
Approximate Weight:	40 tons
Crew:	4
Armament:	105mm main gun /20mm coaxial automatic cannon and one machine gun

Almost 2,000 units of the AMX-30 main battle tanks and variants came off the assembly line before production ceased in the early 1990s. The tank also has served in at least a dozen other armies. *Defense Visual Information Center*

TANK SUSPENSION SYSTEM
A modern tank's ability to maintain high speeds on rough terrain is dependent on not only engine power, but also its suspension system. The suspension system protects the running gear from high forces and makes the ride tolerable for the crew. The addition of heavy dampers (shock absorbers) helps minimizes pitching and rolling of the hull.

The replacement for the AMX-30 main battle tank proved to be the Leclerc main battle tank that entered the French Army inventory in January 1992. *Christophe Vallier*

The French Army currently has about 400 Leclerc main tanks in service, including variants such as an armored recovery vehicle. The United Arab Emirates has 436 units of the Leclerc and variants in service. *Christophe Vallier*

German Tanks

German Tanks

While the senior military leadership of the German Army was somewhat aware of the British Army's efforts to develop tracked vehicles for combat use in World War I, they themselves had little interest in the concept. Even when the British Army deployed 49 tanks into combat in September 1916, the German generals remained unimpressed and considered the newly introduced tanks a short-lived fad. It took until November 1917, when the British Army deployed almost 500 tanks into battle and created widespread panic among the defending German troops that the generals took serious notice and began putting funding into the development of their own tanks.

Despite the newfound interest by the German generals in the fielding of tanks, German industry—badly strained by the existing demands of the war—had little left over capacity to design and build tanks from scratch. Of the many tank designs proposed for use by the German Army in World War I, only one, the A7V heavy tank, made it into combat in very small numbers before the fighting ended with an armistice in November 1918.

Despite the German government signing a treaty in 1919 that allowed them only a very small army and no tanks, the German Army quickly began work in secret on building new tanks. In 1935, the German government began a massive rearmament program that included a large number of tanks for the new and growing German Army. These tanks would range from the Panzer I and II light tanks to the Panzer III and Panzer IV medium tanks. As had occurred in World War I, German industry lacked the ability to build enough tanks to satisfy the military's requirements. This problem would also continue to plague the German Army throughout World War II.

Copied from the only remaining example of an A7V that belongs to an Australian military museum is a modern replica of a German World War I A7V tank. *Andreas Kirchhoff*

The A7V was the only German tank to make it into production during World War I. Twenty-four A7Vs were built compared with the roughly 8,000 tanks built by the British and French in that conflict. *Patton Museum of Cavalry and Armor*

A7V	
Length with main gun forward:	24 feet 1 inch
Width:	10 feet
Height:	10 feet 10 inches
Approximate Weight:	33 tons
Crew:	18
Armament:	57mm main gun and up to seven machine guns

While the German Army inventory of Panzer I through IV tanks proved of sufficient number and capability to play an important part in the invasion and conquest of numerous countries between 1939 and 1940, the German invasion of the Soviet Union in the summer of 1941 provided a rude awakening to the German tankers as the Russians had a new medium tank in their inventory, designated the T-34, which rendered almost the entire inventory of existing German tanks and antitank guns useless in a fortnight.

The German interim response to the Russian T-34 was the upgrading of their existing medium tanks with more powerful main guns and thicker armor. The long-term solution to the T-34 threat was the development and fielding of the Tiger E heavy tank in 1942 and the Panther medium tank in 1943. As the Russians responded with an upgraded T-34 medium tank in 1944 and new heavy tanks, the Germans fielded the Tiger B heavy tank equipped with a more powerful 88mm main gun.

With the conclusion of World War II, the Germans found themselves forbidden by the victors to have either an army or tanks. However, as the relationship between the Soviet Union and their former ally, the

United States, began to chill after World War II, the United States decided to allow and encourage formation of a new West German Army—equipped with American tanks—as a bulwark against Soviet military aggression in Western Europe. The Soviet Union formed the East German Army in 1956 and equipped it with Russian tanks.

Unlike East Germany that was content to employ Russian-designed tanks throughout the Cold War, the West German Army found their American-supplied tanks did not meet their needs and quickly set about fielding their own tanks, the first being the Leopard I main battle tank in the 1960s. The Leopard II main battle tank followed in the 1980s. Both tanks have enjoyed widespread sales success and see service with a large numbers of armies around the world.

Because German industry proved unable to build sufficient numbers of tanks during World War I, they placed a number of captured British tanks into service with German markings as seen here on railroad flatcars. *Patton Museum of Cavalry and Armor*

PANZER I LIGHT TANK	
Length:	13 feet 3 inches
Width:	6 feet 9 inches
Height:	5 feet 8 inches
Approximate Weight:	6 tons
Crew:	2
Armament:	Two machine guns

The initial version of the German Army two-man Panzer I light tank began rolling off assembly lines in 1934. Production continued until 1937 with about 1,500 units completed. *Thomas Anderson*

On display at a modern Spanish Army base is a German Panzer I series light tank. Hitler supplied about 100 to the Nationalist cause during the Spanish Civil War (1936–1939). *Patton Museum of Cavalry and Armor*

544 S   10480 H.

A side view of the German Army's experimental, multi-turreted *Neubaufahrzeug* medium tank. Only five entered service and three saw use in the German military invasion of Norway in 1940. *Patton Museum of Cavalry and Armor*

Production of the three-man Panzer II series light tank began in 1936 and ended in 1940. It disappeared from frontline German Army service by 1943. *Patton Museum of Cavalry and Armor*

A restored example of a Panzer II series light tank, employed by the German Army during World War II, takes part in a public demonstration held by the modern German Army tank museum. *Thomas Anderson*

The four-man Panzer II Luchs (Lynx), of which only 100 came off the production lines between 1943 and 1944, was a highly specialized light reconnaissance tank built for the German Army in World War II. *Tank Museum, Bovington*

Production of the five-man Panzer III series medium tank for the German Army took place between 1937 and 1943, with almost 6,000 units completed. It came with an advanced torsion bar suspension system. *Christophe Vallier*

The Panzer III series medium tank originally showed up on the battlefield with a short-barrel 37mm main gun. It later received a long-barreled 50mm main gun, as seen here. *Chu Hsu*

When the 50mm main gun on the Panzer III series medium tank became obsolete against enemy tanks, the final version showed up with a short-barreled 75mm howitzer that fired a useful shaped-charge antitank warhead. *Richard Hunnicutt*

EARLY MODEL PANZER III MEDIUM TANK	
Length:	18 feet 6 inches
Width:	9 feet 6 inches
Height:	8 feet
Approximate Weight:	21 tons
Crew:	5
Armament:	37mm main gun and two machine guns

The vehicle commander of a Panzer III series medium tank, armed with a short-barrel 75mm main gun, stands on the top of the turret of his tank to survey the surrounding terrain with a pair of binoculars. *Patton Museum of Cavalry and Armor*

(opposite page, top) Originally intended as a fire-support vehicle to deal with enemy towed antitank guns and other defensive fortifications, the first few versions of the five-man Panzer IV medium tank series mounted a short-barrel 75mm howitzer. *Richard Hunnicutt*

(opposite page, bottom) To destroy enemy tanks boasting armor thicker than the main guns on the Panzer III medium tanks could deal with, the Panzer IV series medium tanks was up-gunned with a long-barrel 75mm main gun. *R. Bazalevsky*

MAIN-GUN AMMUNITION
The components of tank main-gun cartridges are the primer, the propelling charge, and the projectile. The primer receives the firing impulse and ignites the propellant. Some primers are percussion caps, such as those seen on small arms ammunition, but most now use an electric primer. A cartridge case normally contains the three components together.

LATE MODEL PANZER IV MEDIUM TANK

Length with main gun forward:	19 feet 5 inches
Width:	9 feet 5 inches
Height:	8 feet 9 inches
Approximate Weight:	26 tons
Crew:	5
Armament:	75mm cannon and two machine guns

The Panzer IV medium tanks first began to appear with a long-barrel high-velocity 75mm main gun in 1942. During World War II, German factories build almost 9,000 units of the Panzer IV series. *David Marian*

What made the German Tiger E heavy tank such a dangerous threat on the battlefield was thick frontal armor and a powerful, high-velocity 88mm main gun derived from an antiaircraft gun design. *Tank Museum, Bovington*

This overhead photograph shows a German Tiger E heavy tank with all crew hatches open. There were three men in the turret and two in the front hull. *Patton Museum of Cavalry and Armor*

Power for the Tiger E heavy tank came from a liquid-cooled gasoline engine that generated 700 horsepower and drove the vehicle to a top speed of 24 miles per hour on a level surface. *Ground Power Magazine*

TIGER E HEAVY TANK

Length with main gun forward:	27 feet
Width:	12 feet 3 inches
Height:	9 feet 4 inches
Approximate Weight:	60 tons
Crew:	5
Armament:	88mm cannon and three machine guns

German factories built only 1,354 units of the Tiger E heavy tank between 1942 and 1944. In comparison, American factories built almost 50,000 units of the Sherman series medium tank between 1942 and 1945. *Patton Museum of Cavalry and Armor*

SLOPING ARMOR
Armor designers try to keep armor surfaces sloping so an incoming projectile will ricochet upward. Another benefit of sloped armor is the increase in areal density. A vertical armor surface hit by a round with a horizontal line of fire defeats a threat based on its thickness alone. A sloped plate appears thicker to an incoming round and possesses a higher areal density. If the slope is high enough, rounds will deflect from the surface rather than penetrate the armor.

Another dangerous threat to Allied tanks in World War II proved to be the Panther medium tank (also known as the Panzer V) equipped with a powerful, high-velocity 75mm main gun and thick, well-sloped frontal armor. *Michael Green*

German factories built about 6,000 units of the Panther series medium tank between January 1943 and April 1945. Due to the haste in which they went into service, early versions suffered serious teething problems. *Christophe Vallier*

PANTHER MEDIUM TANK

Length with main gun forward:	29 feet 1 inch
Width:	10 feet 10 inches
Height:	9 feet 8 inches
Approximate Weight:	49 tons
Crew:	5
Armament:	75mm cannon and three machine guns

MAIN-GUN RIFLING

World War II tank main guns utilized rifling to stabilize projectiles in flight. The spiraling grooves cut into the bore of the gun tube or barrel gave the projectile its spin. A soft metal rotating band on the projectile engaged the rifling as it moved down the gun's bore. The rotating band also sealed expanding propellant gases behind it. Once a projectile left the muzzle of a gun, the spin imparted to it by the rifling kept it aimed at a target. Without that spin, a projectile would tumble erratically.

American soldiers and aircrew members are looking over an abandoned German Panther medium tank stuck on the side of an earthen embankment. Panther tank crews feared American planes more than American tanks. *Patton Museum of Cavalry and Armor*

The 75mm main-gun barrel on the Panther medium tank series was just over 19 feet long. A large muzzle brake at the end of the barrel helped slow down the recoil of the gun when fired. *Christophe Vallier*

German factories managed to build 489 units of the Tiger B heavy tank between January 1944 and March 1945. The armor on the front of the Tiger B turret was over 7 inches thick. *David Marian*

TIGER B HEAVY TANK	
Length with main gun forward:	33 feet 8 inches
Width:	12 feet 3 inches
Height:	10 feet 1 inch
Approximate Weight:	77 tons
Crew:	5
Armament:	88mm main gun and up to three machine guns

(opposite page, top) The replacement for the German Tiger E heavy tank proved to be the Tiger B heavy tank armed with a longer and more powerful 88mm main gun than that found on its predecessor. *Tank Museum, Bovington*

(opposite page, bottom) American soldiers are pictured taking a joy ride on a captured German Tiger B heavy tank. The very wide steel tracks on the vehicle help distribute the tank's weight on the ground. *National Archives*

To assist in the forming of the West German Army in 1955, the U.S. government supplied 1,120 gasoline-powered M47 Patton medium tanks. The M47 tank pictured belongs to the German Army Tank Museum, Munster. *Thomas Anderson*

TANK RECOIL MECHANISM
Recoil is the rearward movement of a tank's main-gun tube and connecting parts after firing, caused by a reaction to the forward motion of a main-gun projectile and hot gases. Counter-recoil is the forward movement of a main-gun tube and connecting parts returning to its prefiring position, called battery, after recoil. A recoil system is a mechanism designed to absorb the energy of recoil gradually and avoid violent movement of the gun mount in the tank.

Alongside the large number of M47 Patton medium tanks supplied to the West German Army in the 1950s, the American government also supplied 1,666 gasoline-powered M48 Patton medium tanks armed with a 90mm main gun. *Thomas Anderson*

Besides the various versions of the American-built Patton series medium tank supplied to the newly formed West German Army in the 1950s, there also arrived a shipment of American-built M41 Walker Bulldog light tanks. *Patton Museum of Cavalry and Armor*

(opposite page, top) To keep their inventory of M48 Patton medium tanks up to date, the West German Army had 650 units upgraded with diesel engines and 105mm main guns between 1978 and 1980. *Frank Schulz*

(opposite page, bottom) The Soviet Union assisted in the forming and equipping of the East German Army in 1956. The first type of tank supplied to the newly formed army was the Soviet Army T-34/85 medium tank. *Christophe Vallier*

Another tank that saw service with the former East German Army, which disappeared with the reunification of the two Germanys in 1990, was the Soviet-designed T-55 series medium tank armed with a 100mm main gun. *Michael Green*

The Soviet-designed PT-76 light tank performed the reconnaissance role for the former East German Army. This amphibious vehicle had a three-man crew and featured a 76mm main gun. *Michael Green*

(opposite page, top) A former East German Army T-72 main battle tank appears in this picture with a mine plow attached. The majority of East German tanks, numbering more than 2,700, went to the scrap dealers or target ranges. *Michael Green*

(opposite page, bottom) The West German Army set the requirements for a German-designed main battle tank in 1956. The result of that requirement proved to be the four-man Leopard I tank armed with a 105mm main gun. *Frank Schulz*

LEOPARD I MAIN BATTLE TANK

Length with main gun forward:	23 feet 3 inches
Width:	10 feet 8 inches
Height:	8 feet 8 inch
Approximate Weight:	44 tons
Crew:	4
Armament:	105mm main gun and two machine guns

After extensive and successful testing of preseries production versions of the Leopard I main battle tank, the West German government ordered 1,500 units of the diesel-powered tank in August 1963. *Patton Museum of Cavalry and Armor*

Posed at the edge of a wooded area is a former Belgian Army Leopard I tank that now belongs to a private collector. The Belgian Army acquired 334 units of the tank beginning in 1968. *Christophe Vallier*

Leopard I tank production for the West German Army took place between 1965 and 1979. While the Leopard I tank is no longer in service with the German Army, it remains in service with other armies. *Michael Green*

MODERN TANK AMMUNITION
Today's tanks typically fire armor-piercing fin-stabilized discarding sabot (APFSDS) at enemy tanks. APFSDS contains no explosives and depends solely on kinetic energy (KE) for penetration. KE is proportional to the product of half the mass times the square of the impact velocity, so a high-density material (typically depleted uranium or tungsten alloy) arriving at the target at the highest possible velocity gives the best results. Fin-stabilized projectiles have inherently low drag, so they retain much of their muzzle velocity even at extended range. The resulting flat trajectory improves hit probability by minimizing time of flight and reducing sensitivity to range error.

Australia Army Leopard I tanks are taking part in a training exercise. Other countries that bought the tank included Canada, Denmark, Greece, Italy, Australia, Norway, Turkey, and the Netherlands. *Defense Visual Information Center*

Pictured is a Canadian Army Leopard I tank in Afghanistan fitted with a mine plow. To increase protection for the four-man crew, the vehicle has additional armor fitted to the vehicle turret and hull. *Canadian Department of National Defense*

The Leopard II tank was not an improved Leopard I tank, but an entirely new tank with improved armor and a 120mm main gun. The Leopard II tank series entered West German Army service in 1979. *Krauss-Maffei*

The Leopard II series main battle tank receives power from a liquid-cooled turbocharged diesel engine that produces 1,500 horsepower and provides the vehicle a 45-mile-per-hour top speed. The vehicle weighs in at about 60 tons. *Krauss-Maffei*

HIGH-EXPLOSIVE ANTITANK (HEAT) ROUND
A typical HEAT round utilizes a shaped explosive contained in a steel case with a copper-lined conical cavity at the front of the detonating charge. This hollow space directs the force of the explosion forward toward the target. Protruding in front of the projectile is often a steel spike, or standoff tube, that allows the explosive to be detonated just before the body of the projectile impacts the target. This feature gives the exploding shaped charge time to form into a jet of superheated metal and gas capable of burning through the target armor.

In order to keep the Leopard II tank up to date when compared with those of other nation's armies, the German Army had the tank continuously upgraded. The latest version is the Leopard 2A5. *Andreas Kirchhoff*

The most easily recognized external feature of the Leopard IIA5 tank compared to the earlier versions of the vehicle are the replaceable wedge-shaped add-on armor blocks, attached to the front of the turret. *Krauss-Maffei*

American Tanks

American Tanks

Because American industry lacked the skill and infrastructure needed to design and build a successful light or heavy tank candidate for use in the closing stages of World War I, the U.S. Army employed French light tanks and British heavy tanks. An American-built copy of the French Renault FT-17 light tank known as the M1917 showed up too late to see combat in World War I, but would serve on with the American military until the 1930s.

Due to funding constraints and disagreements within the U.S. Army on how to employ tanks during the period between World War I and the start of World War II on September 1, 1939, American tank development did not receive a very high priority. It proved to be the successful use of medium tanks by the German Army between 1939 and 1941 that pushed the U.S. Army to pour money and talent into their own medium tank designs. The eventual result of this line of development proved to be the fielding of the M4 series medium tanks, also commonly referred to as the Sherman, of which almost 50,000 were built between 1942 and 1945.

As the most numerous tank built during World War II, the Sherman tank series featured a variety of weapons and received power from a number of different engine types. While a first-rate tank design by 1942 standards, the U.S. Army failed to keep up with the new tank designs fielded by the German Army and the Sherman became obsolete by 1943 standards. Despite its gun and armament shortcomings, it would soldier on with a variety of incremental improvements until the end of the war in Europe in May 1945.

It took the fielding of a small number of 90mm-main-gun-armed M26 Pershing heavy tanks—later reclassified as medium

The Ford Motor Company had designed and built a two-man light tank for use by the U.S. Army during World War I. It failed to meet army requirements and only 15 came off the assembly line. *Michael Green*

tanks—during the last few months of the war in Europe by the U.S. Army to help redress, in a very small way, the battlefield superiority of German tanks. The Pershing would go on to demonstrate its battlefield potential during the Korean War (1950–1953) by easily destroying the Russian-supplied medium tanks used by its North Korean opponent.

To counter the growing threat of a possible Soviet invasion of Western Europe in the early 1950s, spearheaded by thousands of Russian tanks, the U.S. Army sought to improve its tank inventory. The first step was upgrading the M26 Pershing medium tank with a new engine and renaming it the M46 Patton tank. Following an improved M46A1 Patton tank appeared the 90mm-main-gun-armed M47 Patton medium tank. Unhappiness with the M47 soon led to the fielding of the 90mm-main-gun-armed M48 Patton medium tank series. Long-range fire-support for the medium tanks came from the M103 heavy tank series armed with a 120mm main gun.

In reaction to the fielding of new Russian tanks in the 1950s, the U.S. Army decided to field an improved M48 Patton tank armed with a 105mm gun and powered by a diesel engine. Reflecting the various improvements made to the vehicle's design, it became the M60 main battle tank series, which combined the firepower of a heavy tank on a medium tank chassis and entered service in 1959.

The replacement for the M60 tank turned out to be the M1 Abrams tank series, which first came off the production line in 1981. Originally armed with a 105mm main gun it later received a new German-designed 120mm main gun in 1985 and became the M1A1 Abrams tank. Upgraded versions include the M1A2 SEP that first appeared in U.S. Army service in 2001. It is the fifth version of the series and the newest in service.

The M1917 was an improved American copy of the French Renault FT-17 light tank. None made it off the production line in time to see combat with the U.S. Army in World War I. *Michael Green*

Taking part in a training exercise is a U.S. Army M1917 light tank sometime during the 1920s. The vehicle would stay in service with the American military until the late 1930s. *Patton Museum of Cavalry and Armor*

(below) The first U.S. Army heavy tank was the 11-man Mark VIII, intended for use in World War I. It did not go into production until 1920 and disappeared from U.S. Army service in 1932. *Patton Museum of Cavalry and Armor*

M1917 LIGHT TANK

Length:	16 feet
Width:	5 feet 8 inches
Height:	7 feet 6 inches
Approximate Weight:	7.3 tons
Crew:	2
Armament:	37mm cannon or a single machine gun

Because early track designs did not last very long, some tanks, such as the T3 medium tank tested by the U.S. Army in the 1930s, could operate on roads without their tracks. *Patton Museum of Cavalry and Armor*

An M1 combat car belonging to the Cavalry branch of the U.S. Army takes part in a winter training exercise in the late 1930s. The vehicle had a four-man crew and boasted three machine guns. *Patton Museum of Cavalry and Armor*

> **TANKS VS. COMBAT CARS**
> U.S. Army vehicle designations from the 1930s are confusing since the American Congress had given the proponency for tank development to the infantry branch of the U.S. Army. The cavalry branch of the U.S. Army had to call their tanks combat cars as a result. With the forming of the Armored Force in July 1940, this artificial division disappeared.

Pictured on display at the former tank mile at Aberdeen Proving Ground, Maryland, is a four-man, twin-turreted, machine-gun-armed M2A2 light tank, used by the U.S. Army infantry branch in the 1930s. *Dick Hunnicutt*

Belonging to a private collector is this M3 Stuart light tank in U.S. Army markings. The tank was an upgrade of the M2A4 light tank and was supplied to many of America's allies in World War II. *Michael Green*

The M5 Stuart light tank received power from two modified Cadillac gasoline car engines and was an improved version of the earlier M3 series light tanks, with a revised front-hull design. *Michael Green*

All of the American-built M3 and M5 series light tanks had a 37mm main gun, which proved useless against the armor protection on German medium and heavy tanks in World War II. *Christophe Vallier*

A view of the two-man turret on a restored M5 Stuart light tank shows the closed breech end of the 37mm main gun and the tank commander/gunner's seat. *Michael Green*

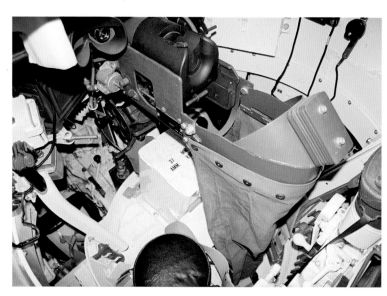

The five-man M24 Chaffee light tank was the replacement for the M5 light tank series and featured a 75mm main gun and three machine guns. *Michael Green*

M5 LIGHT TANK	
Length:	15 feet 9 inches
Width:	7 feet 5 inches
Height:	7 feet 6 inches
Approximate Weight:	17 tons
Crew:	4
Armament:	37mm cannon and three machine guns

The U.S. Army began thinking about a new tank small and light enough for transport by aircraft in early 1941. The result of this interest proved to be the M22 Locust, with a 37mm main gun. *Christophe Vallier*

(opposite page, top) Reflecting pre–World War II U.S. Army tank design philosophy is this six-man M2A1 medium tank armed with a turret-mounted 37mm main gun and seven machine guns. *Patton Museum of Cavalry and Armor*

(opposite page, bottom) Following the M2A1 medium tank into U.S. Army service was the M3 series medium tank armed with a turret-mounted 37mm gun and a front-hull-mounted 75mm with limited traverse. *Michael Green*

M3 MEDIUM TANK	
Length:	18 feet 6 inches
Width:	8 feet 11 inches
Height:	10 feet 3 inches
Approximate Weight:	30 tons
Crew:	6–7
Armament:	Two cannons (37mm and 75mm), three machine guns

Desiring a medium tank armed with a 75mm main gun in a 360-degree traversable turret, U.S. Army introduced the M4 series tank, often referred to as the Sherman. *Christophe Vallier*

WHERE THE "SHERMAN" IN SHERMAN TANK CAME FROM
The American military did not begin assigning official nicknames to its tanks until January 1945. It was the British Army that assigned the official nickname "General Sherman," normally shortened to just "Sherman," to the large number of American-designed and -built M4 series medium tanks shipped to Great Britain beginning in 1942, as part of a military aid program known as Lend Lease.

The picture taken from the loader's position on an M4A1 version of the Sherman tank shows the driver's seat and controls on the left and the vehicle's transmission on the right. *Michael Green*

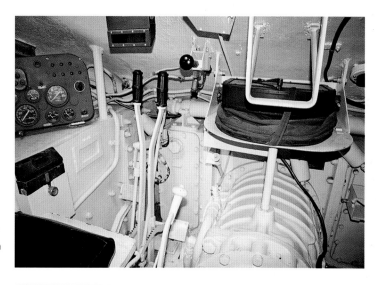

Pictured is an M4A3 version of the Sherman tank. While all Sherman tanks featured cast homogenous-armor turrets, some had hulls constructed out of rolled homogenous-armor plates welded together, as does the vehicle shown. *Michael Green*

M4A1 MEDIUM TANK

Length:	19 feet 3 inches
Width:	8 feet 6 inches
Height:	9 feet
Approximate Weight:	33 tons
Crew:	5
Armament:	75mm cannon and three machine guns

Many of the M4 Sherman medium tanks built had a cast homogenous-armor hull as seen here on this M4A1 version of the vehicle. Tests eventually showed the U.S. Army that rolled homogenous was superior. *Michael Green*

A low-rate production version of the M4 Sherman series medium tanks was the M4A3E2 assault tank, nicknamed the Jumbo. It differed from the standard Sherman because of more armor protection. *David Marian*

M4A3W(76) HVSS SHERMAN TANK

Length with main gun forward:	24 feet 6 inches
Width:	9 feet 8 inches
Height:	9 feet 6 inches
Approximate Weight:	37 tons
Crew:	5
Armament:	76mm cannon and three machine guns

American factories began production of a new second-generation version of the Sherman medium tanks in 1944, which featured a wider track suspension system and a new long-barreled 76mm main gun. *Patton Museum of Cavalry and Armor*

Another tank destroyer fielded by the American military during World War II was the M18, sometimes referred to as the Hellcat. The four-man tank destroyer mounted a 76mm main gun. *Michael Green*

(opposite page, top) A number of tank destroyers appeared in American military service during World War II, one of them being the M10 armed with a 3-inch main gun and based on the Sherman tank chassis. *Christophe Vallier*

(opposite page, bottom) Unhappiness with the poor penetrative performance of the 3-inch gun on the M10 tank destroyer led to the U.S. Army adoption of the M36 tank destroyer armed with a more powerful 90mm main gun. *Christophe Vallier*

The U.S. Army decided to begin development of a new medium tank in 1942. Almost three years of hard work resulted in the fielding of the 90mm-main-gun-armed M26 Pershing tank in 1945. *Bob Fleming*

Looking through the vehicle commander's hatch on an M26A1 Pershing tank is the massive breech end of the 90mm main gun on the left and the gunner's seat and controls on the right. *Michael Green*

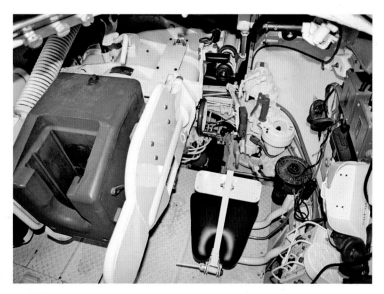

One of the American heavy tanks designed during World War II was the T-29 armed with a 105mm main gun. The army had originally ordered 1,200 units in March 1945, but later cancelled the order. *Michael Green*

The M46 Patton medium tank was a modernized M26 Pershing medium tank with an automatic transmission and a more powerful gasoline engine. The 90mm main gun from the Pershing series remained. *Patton Museum of Cavalry and Armor*

M46 PATTON MEDIUM TANK

Length with main gun forward:	27 feet 8 inches
Width:	11 feet 5 inches
Height:	10 feet
Approximate Weight:	49 tons
Crew:	5
Armament:	90mm cannon and three machine guns

The outbreak of the Korean War (1950–1953) caused the U.S. Army to field a new family of tanks, including a light, medium, and heavy tank. The M41 Walker Bulldog tank filled the light tank role. *Michael Green*

Production of the 90mm-main-gun-armed M47 Patton tank began in June 1951. The five-man tank had a pronounced rear-turret bustle that contained the vehicle's radios. *Patton Museum of Cavalry and Armor*

M103 HEAVY TANK

Length with main gun forward:	37 feet 4 inches
Width:	11 feet 7 inches
Height:	11 feet 8 inches
Approximate Weight:	62.5 tons
Crew:	5
Armament:	120mm cannon and two machine guns

The 120mm-main-gun-armed M103 heavy tank was to support the U.S. Army's medium tanks in battle by destroying Soviet Army heavy tanks, such as the IS-III Stalin armed with a 122mm main gun. *TACOM Historical Office*

WHERE THE "PATTON" IN PATTON TANKS CAME FROM
The "Patton" in Patton tanks came from the U.S. Army's decision to honor the memory of one of its best-known and famous leaders, General George S. Patton, who led his 3rd Army—spearheaded by Sherman tanks—to Victory against Nazi Germany during World War II. To the newspapers of the day he was nicknamed "Old Blood and Guts."

Painted in a desert camouflage scheme are two U.S. Marine Corps 90mm-main-gun-armed M48A3 Patton medium tanks taking part in a 1976 training exercise. The M48 series had only a four-man crew. *Defense Visual Information Center*

The replacement for the 90mm-main-gun-armed M48 Patton series medium tank and the 120mm-main-gun-armed M103 heavy tank proved to be the M60 main battle tank (MBT) armed with a 105mm main gun. *Dick Hunnicutt*

M60A1 MAIN BATTLE TANK

Length with main gun forward:	31 feet
Width:	11 feet 9 inches
Height:	10 feet 7 inches
Approximate Weight:	52.5 tons
Crew:	4
Armament:	105mm cannon and two machine guns

Unhappiness with the armor protection level on the rounded turret of the original M60 tank led to adoption of a more thickly armored elongated turret on the M60A1 tank seen here. *Defense Visual Information Center*

A shortage of M60A1 tanks in the 1970s led the U.S. Army to take older-model M48 series medium Patton tanks and replace their 90mm main guns with 105mm main guns. They then became the M48A5 Patton tank. *Michael Green*

A vehicle commander on a U.S. Army M60A3 tank holds the powered turret traverse handle with his right hand. On his head, he wears a combat vehicle crewmember (CVC) helmet fitted with headphones and a microphone. *Defense Visual Information Center*

TRACERS
Almost all tank ammunition features tracers. Kinetic energy ammunition is particularly hard to sense (spot) when it misses the target since it does not explode on contact with the ground, so tracers are useful. Night photos of tracers often appear with squiggles caused by vibration of the camera from the muzzle blast.

Visible is the fireball from the firing of a 105mm main gun mounted on an M60A1 tank during a nighttime training exercise, as well as the tracer elements from other projectiles in flight.
Defense Visual Information Center

The M60A2 tank featured a short-barreled 152mm main gun that was also capable of accurately firing a large antitank missile, known as the Shillelagh, out to a range of almost 2 miles. *TACOM Historical Office*

The crew of an M551 Sheridan has removed all the various rounds and antitank missiles that are normally stored within the vehicle. The Sheridan mounted the same 152mm gun/antitank missile launcher as found on the M60A2 tank. *Defense Visual Information Center*

Inside the turret of an M551 Sheridan are some of the Shillelagh antitank missiles on the left and the open breech of the 152mm gun/antitank missile launcher on the right. *Michael Green*

M551 SHERIDAN LIGHT TANK

Length:	20 feet 7 inches
Width:	9 feet 7 inches
Height:	9 feet 7 inches
Approximate Weight:	17 tons
Crew:	4
Armament:	152mm combination gun/missile launcher and two machine guns

When the Sheridans became obsolete, they went on to become vague copies of Soviet Army tanks and other armored fighting vehicles for training purposes and were called VisMods. The M551 pictured represents a Soviet Army infantry-fighting vehicle. *Defense Visual Information Center*

To help protect their M60A1 tanks from infantry hand-held antitank weapons, the U.S. Marine Corps began affixing explosive reactive armor (ERA) tiles to the exterior of their hulls and turrets. *Defense Visual Information Center*

To keep the M60A1 tank up to date, the U.S. Army installed a laser range finder, new fire-control computer, and a thermal sleeve on the barrel. These improvements turned it into the M60A3 tank seen here. *Defense Visual Information Center*

The U.S. Army set about replacing the M60 series beginning in the early 1970s. The result of their work was the M1 Abrams tank armed with a 105mm main gun. *TACOM Historical Office*

M1 Abrams series tank hulls proceed down the assembly line. Production of the original 60-ton, 105mm-gun-armed version of the M1 Abrams series tank began in 1980. *General Dynamics Land Systems*

M1A1 ABRAMS TANK

Length with main gun forward:	32 feet
Width:	12 feet 4 inches
Height:	9 feet 5 inches
Approximate Weight:	63 tons
Crew:	4
Armament:	120mm cannon and three machine guns

The 63-ton M1A1 version of the Abrams first rolled off the production line in 1985. It featured a German-designed 120mm main gun and more armor protection. *Defense Visual Information Center*

The vehicle commander of a U.S. Army 70-ton M1A2 system enhancement package (SEP) version of the Abrams tank looks out through his vision blocks on his cupola. The SEP is the newest Abrams tank version. *Department of Defense*

The sophistication of the Abrams fire-control system virtually assures first-round kills on any target within 2 miles. Target hits at even farther distances are not uncommon. *Defense Visual Information Center*

THERMAL IMAGING SIGHTS
Thermal imaging sighting systems are sophisticated heat detection devices that provide images of objects on a monitor inside a tank. Since the device sees emitted heat energy and does not use visible light, it provides a tank crew gunner the ability to identify and engage targets, even on the darkest of nights.

The loader on this original 105mm-main-gun-armed version of the M1 Abrams series tank is ready to shove a main gun round into the breech of the vehicle's cannon. *Defense Visual Information Center*

On a tank firing range in the Middle East, an M1A1 Abrams tank has just fired a main-gun round. The projectile will travel downrange at over a mile per second. *Defense Visual Information Center*

Russian Tanks

Russian Tanks

During the Russian Civil War (1917–1922), the Red Army captured some of the French and British tanks supplied to their opponents, the White Army, and turned them against their former users. In the aftermath of the Russian Civil War, the Red Army set about the development of their own tanks, which was aided by the massive industrialization of the Russian economy beginning in the late 1920s, continuing into the 1930s.

While early Red Army tank designs were reversed-engineered or improved copies of foreign tanks, by 1940, they had amassed enough experience to come up with their own tank designs.

When the German Army invaded the Soviet Union in the summer of 1941, they found themselves confronting the Red Army, which possessed an inventory of over 23,000 tanks (more than the rest of the world combined). Fortunately, for the German Army, most of the Red Army tanks were obsolete and poorly maintained. However, among this mass of steel were almost 1,000 T-34/76 medium tanks, first introduced into Red Army service in 1940.

With outstanding mobility and protected by thick, well-sloped armor for its time and armed with a 76mm main gun, the T-34/76 made every tank and antitank gun in the German Army obsolete overnight. To counter this tank, German tank designers entered into a gun-armor race with the Red Army tank designers that continued until the Germans surrendered in May 1945.

While the Germans came up with the Panther and Tiger tanks in response to the T-34/76 tank, Russian industry did not rest upon their laurels and fielded an improved T-34 medium tank in 1944, armed with an

Another British tank supplied to the White Army to fight the Red Army during the Russian Civil War was the Whippet medium tank. Armed only with machine guns, the Whippet had two engines. *Michael Green*

85mm main gun and designated T-34/85. In conjunction with the up-armed T-34/85, Russia also introduced the IS-II Joseph Stalin heavy tank, armed with a 122mm main gun, in 1944.

Even before Germany surrendered, Russian tank designers were working on their next generation of tanks. The most important and numerous would be the T-54/55 medium tank series armed with a 100mm main gun. The first prototypes of the T-54 appeared in 1946, and the T-55 in 1956. With license-built foreign copies of the T-54/55 series tank figured in, estimates are that over 100,000 units of the vehicle have come off the assembly line, making it the most numerous tank series ever built.

Due to the introduction of the American M60 main battle tank into Western Europe in 1960, armed with a 105mm main gun, Russian tank designers took a lengthened T-55 chassis and added a new enlarged turret mounting a 115mm main gun to it. The upgraded T-55 medium tank received the designation T-62 main battle tank. Over 20,000 units of the T-62 came across assembly lines between 1962 and 1978.

The initial replacement for the T-54/55 medium tank series and the T-62 main battle tank in Soviet Army service (the

During the Russian Civil War, the British and French Armies supplied the White Army, fighting the Bolshevik Red Army, with about 130 tanks; these included the British Mark V heavy tank pictured here. *Vladimir Yakubov*

former Red Army) was the T-64 main battle tank armed with a powerful 125mm main gun. Production of the tank began in 1973 and ended in 1987, with about 8,000 units built. Never exported, the costly T-64 had some design problems that resulted in the Soviet Army going ahead with production of a lower-cost main battle tank designated the T-72 in 1971, armed with the same 125mm main gun mounted on the T-64. Over 20,000 units of the T-72 series tank have come off the production line, both Russian- and license-built copies.

Another alternative to the T-64 taken into Soviet Army service was the 125mm-main-gun-equipped T-80 main battle tank, which entered production in 1976. Over 4,500 units of the T-80 series tanks came off the assembly line for the Soviet Army and foreign customers before production ended in the late 1990s. With the collapse of the Soviet Union in 1991, the Soviet Army became the Russian Federation Army. The newest tank in the Russian Federation Army is the T-90, a modernized version of the T-72, introduced into service in 1994.

The Red Army captured a number of French Army FT-17 light tanks from the White Army during the Russian Civil War. Fifteen rebuilt examples became the Freedom Fighter Lenin light tank, or the "M" light tank. *Vladimir Yakubov*

The Red Army used the T-18 light tank between 1928 and 1942. The tank mounted both a 37mm main gun and two machine guns and was an improved version of the French Army FT-17 light tank. *Vladimir Yakubov*

In Finish Army colors is this former two-man Red Army T-26 light tank armed with a 45mm main gun. The T-26 was almost an exact copy of a British light tank design acquired by the Red Army in 1930. *Tank Museum, Bovington*

A destroyed Red Army T-26 light tank awaits the scrap merchant dealers. Russian factories built 4,500 units of the T-26 series tanks between 1932 and 1939. *Patton Museum of Cavalry and Armor*

T-26 LIGHT TANK

Length:	15 feet 2 inches
Width:	8 feet
Height:	6 feet 10 inches
Approximate Weight:	9 tons
Crew:	3
Armament:	45mm cannon and two machine guns

THE PURPOSE OF DRIVE SPROCKETS

Drive sprockets, one on either side of a tank's hull, receive their power from a tank's engine by way of the transmission. Large gears in the final drives reduce the transmission speed and increase the torque at the sprockets. The tracks are lifted off the ground at the rear of the vehicle after the road wheels have driven over it. The tracks are under the control of the sprockets, which deliver the "tractive effort" between the tank and the ground.

The Red Army T-37 light amphibious tank was a copy of a British tank bought by the Russians in 1930. About 1,200 units of the T-37 entered service with the Red Army between 1933 and 1936. *Patton Museum of Cavalry and Armor*

A Red Army light tank built during World War II was the two-man T-60 mounting a 20mm automatic cannon. Russian factories built over 6,000 units of the T-60 during the war. *Vladimir Yakubov*

During a public demonstration, volunteers are driving around a World War II–era T-70 light tank in Red Army markings. Over 8,000 T-70s rolled off the assembly lines between 1942 and 1943. *R. Bazalevsky*

The BT-7 fast tank was the culmination of a series of Red Army light tanks based on the suspension system developed by American inventor J. W. Christie. The three-tank had a 45mm main gun. *Patton Museum of Cavalry and Armor*

BT-7 FAST TANK	
Length:	18 feet 7 inches
Width:	7 feet 6 inches
Height:	7 feet 11 inches
Approximate Weight:	15 tons
Crew:	3
Armament:	45mm cannon and one machine gun

Developed between 1939 and 1941, the T-50 light tank was the planned replacement for the Red Army T-26 and BT series light tanks. Production problems doomed the project with only 63 units constructed. *Vladimir Yakubov*

Taking part in a World War II Red Army parade is a T-28 medium tank. The six-man tank had three turrets, one armed with a 76.2mm main gun and the other two with machine guns.
Patton Museum of Cavalry and Armor

RUNNING GEAR
The components external to the hull (final drives, sprockets, idler wheels, tracks, and road wheels) make up a tank's running gear. The idler wheels, one for each track at the front of the vehicle (for rear drive configurations) or at the rear (for front drive configurations), reverse the direction of the tracks at the unpowered end of the vehicle.

German soldiers pose in front of a knocked out Red Army T-35 heavy tank equipped with three turrets. One armed with a 76.2mm gun and the other two with 45mm guns. Only 61 went into service. *Patton Museum of Cavalry and Armor*

T-35 HEAVY TANK	
Length:	31 feet 10 inches
Width:	10 feet 6 inches
Height:	11 feet 3 inches
Approximate Weight:	55 tons
Crew:	11
Armament:	One 76.2mm cannon, two 45mm cannons, and six machine guns

Buried under a blanket of snow is the sole example of an experimental Red Army SMK heavy tank, destroyed during the Russo-Finnish War (1939–1940). The design of the SMK led to the KV series heavy tanks. *Patton Museum of Cavalry and Armor*

KV-1 HEAVY TANK

Length:	20 feet 7 inches
Width:	10 feet 2 inches
Height:	7 feet 11 inches
Approximate Weight:	52 tons
Crew:	5
Armament:	76.2mm cannon and three machine guns

The KV series heavy tanks began with some Russian engineers deciding that the SMK heavy tank would be better off with only one turret rather than two. This resulted in the KV-1 heavy tank. *Michael Green*

The ungainly-looking Red Army KV-2 heavy tank was a KV-1 heavy tank hull fitted with a large box-like turret armed with a 152mm howitzer. The intended target was enemy defensive positions. *Patton Museum of Cavalry and Armor*

Workhorse of the Red Army armored forces during World War II was the four-man T-34/76 medium tank armed with a 76.2mm main gun. Russian factories built around 34,000 units between 1940 and 1944. *Michael Green*

T-34/85 MEDIUM TANK

Length:	24 feet 7 inches
Width:	9 feet 7 inches
Height:	7 feet 10 inches
Approximate Weight:	35 tons
Crew:	5
Armament:	85mm cannon and two machine guns

(opposite page, top) The Red Army T-34/76 tank commander also had to perform the role of loader, which made it much harder for him to keep track of what was going on outside his vehicle. *Michael Green*

(opposite page, bottom) To counter the introduction of German tanks boasting thicker armor protection, the Red Army introduced the five-man T-34/85 medium tank into service in 1944, armed with an 85mm main gun. *Michael Green*

Russian factories built about 23,000 units of the T-34/85 medium tank during World War II, with another roughly 22,000 coming off the factory floor between July 1945 and 1950. *Andreas Kirchhoff*

The front hull crew compartment of a T-34/85 medium tank with the driver on the left and the machine gunner on the right; in the turret of the tank would be the vehicle commander, gunner, and loader. *Michael Green*

The Red Army replacement for the KV-1 heavy tank was the four-man IS-2 heavy tank armed with a 122mm main gun. It first saw action in April 1944. Russian factories built about 4,000 between 1943 and 1945. *Christophe Vallier*

IS-3 HEAVY TANK

Length:	32 feet 9 inches
Width:	10 feet 6 inches
Height:	8 feet 11 inches
Approximate Weight:	51 tons
Crew:	4
Armament:	122mm cannon and two machine guns

Arriving too late to see combat with the Red Army in World War II was the four-man IS-3 Stalin heavy tank armed with a 122mm main gun. The tank would last in service through the 1950s. *R. Bazalevsky*

In support of the Soviet Union's fight against Nazi Germany in World War II, both the British and Americans supplied thousands of tanks to the Red Army. These included almost 5,500 M4 series medium tanks. *Patton Museum of Cavalry and Armor*

Soviet factories built about 35,000 units of the four-man T-54 series medium tank between 1946 and 1958. In addition, roughly 25,000 license-built foreign copies were made, with China building the largest number. *Michael Green*

The T-54 series medium tank, armed with a 100mm main gun, was widely adopted by those countries that fell within the sphere of interest of the Soviet Union. Pictured are Polish Army T-54 medium tanks on parade. *Patton Museum of Cavalry and Armor*

Among the many armies that acquired a large number of T-54 series medium tanks was the Iraqi Army. The T-54 tank pictured suffered destruction at the hands of the American military in 1991. *Defense Visual Information Center*

Taking part in a training exercise for the American-supported Iraqi Army is a modernized Chinese-made copy of the Soviet-designed T-54 medium tank, referred to as the Type 69-11 main battle tank. *Department of Defense*

The T-55 medium tank was an upgraded T-54 medium tank that retained the predecessor's 100mm main gun, but had the ability to fight in a nuclear-contaminated environment. The T-55 pictured is in Czech Army markings. *Michael Green*

T-55 MEDIUM TANK
Length:	29 feet 6 inches
Width:	10 feet 9 inches
Height:	7 feet 10 inches
Approximate Weight:	40 tons
Crew:	4
Armament:	100mm cannon and two machine guns

These two Chinese-made copies of the T-54/55 medium tank, designated the T-59 II main battle tank, are armed with a 105mm main gun. The gun is a copy of a British-designed 105mm gun. *Defense Visual Information Service*

TANK CREW POSITIONS
Medium and heavy tanks of World War II and shortly thereafter generally tended to have a crew of five men, with the vehicle commander, gunner, and loader in the turret and the driver and assistant driver/machine gunner in the front hull. On German tanks of World War II, the front hull machine gunner was also the radioman. After World War II, the assistant drivers/machine gunners disappeared on most tank designs, leaving only four men in the tanks.

China's military industrial complex has continued to refine their versions of the T-54/55 medium tank series. Pictured in Pakistani Army service is the Chinese-built Type 85 II main battle tank armed with a 125mm main gun. *Tank Museum, Bovington*

On display at a museum is this example of an early prototype of the post–World War II T-10 heavy tank armed with a 122mm main gun. Production began in the early 1950s and ended in 1962. *Vladimir Yakubov*

Used as a reconnaissance vehicle by the Soviet Army was the PT-76 light amphibious tank, armed with a 76mm main gun. Propulsion in the water came from a hydro jet system. *Michael Green*

PT-76 AMPHIBIOUS LIGHT TANK	
Length:	25 feet
Width:	10 feet 4 inches
Height:	7 feet 2 inches
Approximate Weight:	15 tons
Crew:	3
Armament:	76mm cannon and one machine gun

A Russian Naval infantryman (counterpart of the U.S. Marines) poses in front of his PT-76 amphibious light tank. It was widely exported to other countries' armies and the Chinese Army employs a copy designated the Type 60 or 63. *Defense Visual Information Service*

This photograph shows the interior of the turret on a restored PT-76 amphibious light tank owned by a private collector. Soviet factories built about 7,000 units of the vehicle between 1953 and 1969. *Michael Green*

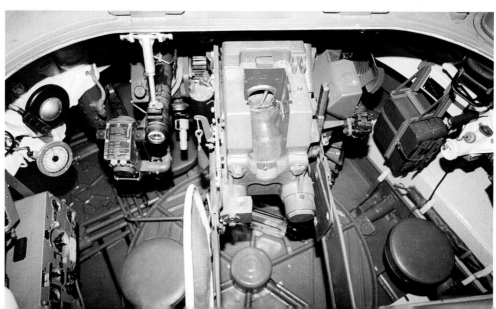

The T-62 main battle tank, armed with a 115mm smoothbore main gun, was a lengthened version of the T-55 medium tank with a new turret and intended to replace the heavy tanks in the Soviet Army inventory. *Defense Visual Information Service*

THE ADVANTAGES OF SMOOTHBORE TANK MAIN GUNS

Smoothbore tank guns have some advantages over rifled tank main guns. They can withstand higher pressure, are cheaper to build, and do not wear out as quickly. For the same explosive charge, the muzzle velocity of a smoothbore gun is higher because it does not waste energy to engrave the rotating bands and to spin the projectile as in a rifled tank gun. Because modern tank gun projectiles are fin stabilized, they do not need to spin in flight.

(opposite page, top) An internal explosion has ruptured the bottom hull plate of this burned out Iraqi Army T-62 main battle tank and knocked the vehicle's turret ajar. *Defense Visual Information Service*

(opposite page, bottom) Tanks are expensive to replace every few years. Like most armies, the Soviet Army continuously upgraded its older-generation tanks to keep them in service. The T-62 pictured has extra armor on the front of the turret. *R. Bazalevsky*

Entering service with the Soviet Army in the 1960s was the T-64 main battle tank armed with a 125mm main gun. It featured an auto-loader that did away with the need for a human loader. *Tank Museum, Bovington*

Pictured at a military museum is a T-64 main battle tank with explosive reactive armor (ERA) tiles on the turret and hull. The T-64 weighed about 46 tons and had a top speed of almost 50 miles per hour. *Bob Fleming*

Painted in United Nations (UN) white is a Russian-designed T-72 main battle tank. It mounts a 125mm main gun and has only a three-man crew because a mechanical loader replaced the human loader. *Defense Visual Information Center*

T-72 MAIN BATTLE TANK

Length with main gun forward:	31 feet 3 inches
Width:	12 feet 9 inches
Height:	7 feet 3 inches
Approximate Weight:	50 tons
Crew:	3
Armament:	125mm cannon and two machine guns

Photographed running at high speed is a T-72 main battle tank covered with explosive reactive armor (ERA) tiles that will dissipate and deflect incoming antitank missiles or projectiles. *R. Bazalevsky*

About 10,000 units of the T-72 main battle tank series remain in the inventory of the Russian Federation Army. Built under license in five other countries besides Russia, the T-72 serves in at least 30 armies. *Tank Museum, Bovington*

(opposite page, top) Developed for use by the Soviet Army in the 1980s, the T-80 series main battle tanks now serve with the Russian Federation Army. Like the T-64 and T-72 tanks, it has a 125mm main gun and an auto-loader. *Tank Museum, Bovington*

(opposite page, bottom) The Russian Federation Army retains an inventory of 4,500 units of the T-80 series main battle tanks. There are also a small number of T-80s in service with Belarus and the Ukraine. *Tank Museum, Bovington*

Tanks from Other Nations

Tanks from Other Nations

The design and building of tanks is restricted to those first-world industrial nations that are willing to invest a massive amount of time and funding needed to produce a product that has no practical value other than wartime use and requires constant updating to keep from becoming obsolete. This has pushed most armies to adopt into service the tanks designed and developed by the Big Five: the British, French, Germans, Americans, and Russians.

While some armies may modify the tanks acquired from the Big Five or license-build them, a few have taken to designing and building their own tanks to become independent of outside supplies. Czech industry was in the forefront of this trend in Europe before World War II. They designed and built a number of light and medium tank designs, which served with a variety of nations before and during World War II.

Prior to World War II, one of the largest tank builders was the Japanese, who had become aware of the impact the tank had on the fighting in Western Europe during World War I. The Japanese Army acquired both British and French tanks after World War I to help quick-start their own tank industry by copying some of the design features.

In the mid-1920s, Japanese industry had acquired enough experience to begin designing and building their own tanks. By 1939, the year World War II started, the Japanese Army had over 2,000 tanks, making it the fourth-largest tank force at the time, lagging behind only the Russian, French, and German inventories.

During World War II, Japanese industry was hard-pressed by the demands of building ships and planes and could not keep pace with the rapid advances made by other nations in tank designs and quickly

With experience gained with license-building small light tanks of British design after World War I, the Czech armament industry decided to build their own tanks. The LT-35 light tank went into service in 1937. *Michael Green*

fell behind in both quality and quantity. When the Japanese Army, known as the Japanese Self Defense Force, reestablished itself in the 1950s, it was equipped with American tanks.

While the first Japanese-designed and -built tank after World War II, designated the Type 61 main battle tank, proved heavily influenced by the design of the American M47 Patton medium tank, the next Japanese Army tank, the Type 74 main battle tank, was an indigenous designed and built tank. The only exception was the tank's 105mm main gun, which was a British-designed weapon built under license in Japan. The replacement for the Type 74 was the Type 90, which entered Japanese Army service in 1991. Like the Type 74, the Type 90 was Japanese designed and built. However, it mounts a license-built, German-designed 120mm main gun.

The Israeli Army has a long history of modifying the tanks they have acquired from a variety of sources—designed and built by the Big Five—to suit its own needs. This is partly due to Israel being a very small

Unhappiness with the LT-35 light tank led the Czech Army to buy the LT-38 light tank, which entered service in 1938. Both tanks had four-man crews and the armament consisted of a 37mm main gun. *Patton Museum of Cavalry and Armor*

country without the financial and industrial resources in the past to design and build a tank from the ground up. This changed in 1979, when the Israeli Army introduced the world to their new main battle tank, named the Chariot (Merkava in Hebrew).

Originally armed with a British-designed 105mm main gun, the later versions of the Merkava tank feature a 120mm main gun designed and built in Israel. The only major component of the tank that comes from an outside source is the American-designed and -built diesel engine.

One feature that makes the Merkava such an interesting tank is the placement of the engine in the vehicle's front hull and the turret in the rear of the hull. This is just the traditional opposite of almost all the tanks built since World War I that feature the engine in the rear hull and the turret in the middle. The Israeli Army's decision to have the engine in the front hull of the Merkava reflected their priority on providing the maximum amount of protection for the crew, a great deal of which comes from the engine placement.

Czechoslovakia fell under Nazi rule in 1938, which led to the disbanding of the Czech Army and their equipment passing into the hands of the German Army. Pictured is a Czech LT-38 with German markings. *Frank Schulz*

The Swiss Army acquired a license-built modified copy of the Czech Army LT-38 light tank before World War II. In Swiss Army service, it received the designation *Panzerwagen 39*. *Andreas Kirchhoff*

LT-38 LIGHT TANK	
Length:	14 feet 11 inches
Width:	7 feet
Height:	7 feet 7 inches
Approximate Weight:	11 tons
Crew:	4
Armament:	37mm cannon and two machine guns

Hungarian Army units employed a license-built, Czech-designed medium tank, which they called the Turan, during World War II. Armed with a 47mm main gun, it had a crew of five men. *Tank Museum, Bovington*

M-13/40 LIGHT TANK
Length:	16 feet 2 inches
Width:	7 feet 3 inches
Height:	7 feet 10 inches
Approximate Weight:	15 tons
Crew:	4
Armament:	47mm cannon and three machine guns

The best Italian tank of World War II proved to be the four-man M-13/40 medium tank armed with a 47mm main gun. Italian industry built 625 units of the M-13/40 between 1940 and 1942. *Christophe Vallier*

Entering into production in 1934 for the Japanese Army was the three-man Type 95 light tank armed with a 47mm main gun. Over 1,000 units of the vehicle rolled out of Japanese factories through 1945. *Michael Green*

Japanese industry also came up with an amphibious version of the Type 95 light tank for the Japanese Navy, which wanted it for their naval infantry units. It had a water speed of 6 miles per hour. *Patton Museum of Cavalry and Armor*

The Type 4 heavy tank was a lengthened and heavier version of the original Japanese Army Type 97 medium tank armed with a 75mm main gun. Only six showed up before World War II ended. *Patton Museum of Cavalry and Armor*

(opposite page, top) The four-man Japanese Army Type 89 medium tank featured a 47mm main gun. The 13-ton tank had a top speed of 17 miles per hour and entered service in 1934. *Richard Hunnicutt*

(opposite page, bottom) A replacement for the Japanese Army Type 89 medium tank turned out to be the Type 97 medium tank. The vehicle pictured is a late-war example of the series known as the Type 97 (Special). *Richard Hunnicutt*

TANK TURRETS
A tank's turret sits on a turret ring, which forms part of a tank's hull. The turret can be rotated by the gunner or vehicle commander using a power-operated system or a manual one. These controls allow the tank turret crew to fire the turret-mounted weapons in any direction when the tank is stationary or moving (with modern tanks). A tank's main gun turns with the turret, but as the gun elevates it moves independently of the turret.

The first post–World War II tank to enter the re-formed Japanese Army, known as the Japanese Self Defense Force, was the Type 61 main battle tank. Japanese factories built 500 units of the tank. *Mitsuo Yaguchi*

Design work on the Type 74 main battle tank began for the Japanese Self Defense Force in the 1960s. It was a replacement for the aging Type 61 main battle tank and entered production in the early 1970s. *Mitsuo Yaguchi*

TYPE 61 MAIN BATTLE TANK	
Length:	20 feet 8 inches
Width:	9 feet 8 inches
Height:	10 feet 4 inches
Approximate Weight:	38 tons
Crew:	4
Armament:	90mm cannon and two machine guns

Entering into service for the Japanese Self Defense Force in 1991 was the three-man Type 90 main battle tank armed with a German-designed 120mm main gun. It was the replacement for the Type 74 tank. *Mitsuo Yaguchi*

Faced with an undependable supply of British tanks early in World War II, the Australia Army sought out a locally produced tank. That vehicle turned out to be the Sentinel tank seen here. *Tank Museum, Bovington*

Early in World War II, Canada designed and built a medium tank, called the Ram, based on the suspension system of the American M3 medium tank. The tank pictured is the Ram II. *Patton Museum of Cavalry and Armor*

A South Korean Army K1 main battle tank armed with a 105mm main gun rolls off a U.S. Navy landing craft. The tank was American-designed, but built in South Korea. It entered service in 1985. *Defense Visual Information Center*

The Panzer 68 is a Swiss-designed and -built main battle tank armed with a British-designed 105mm main gun and powered by a German-designed diesel engine that gives the vehicle a top speed of 34 miles per hour. *Andreas Kirchhoff*

PANZER 68 MAIN BATTLE TANK

Length:	22 feet 8 inches
Width:	10 feet 4 inches
Height:	9 feet
Approximate Weight:	43 tons
Crew:	4
Armament:	105mm cannon and two machine guns

Entering into Swedish Army service in 1966 was the turretless S-tank. The main armament of the three-man vehicle was a 105mm main gun aimed by turning the entire vehicle. *Michael Green*

The amphibious IKV-91 tank destroyer was fielded by the Swedish Army in 1975 and performed all the reconnaissance duties traditionally performed by light tanks. The four-man tank boasted a 90mm main gun. *David Marian*

Belonging to a private collection is this example of a former Israeli Army M1 Super Sherman. The tank featured a World War II–vintage 76.2mm main gun, which was obsolete by postwar standards. *Michael Green*

The Israeli Army's first attempt at prolonging the service life of its inventory of Sherman tanks involved the mounting of a postwar-designed French 75mm gun into a modified Sherman turret. The vehicle became the M50. *Robert Manasherob*

The final version of the Sherman tank in Israeli Army service featured a French-designed and -built 105mm main gun in a modified turret. Tanks so equipped received the designation M51. *Israeli Army*

The mainstay of the Israeli Army's first line tank inventory up through it's 1967 Six-Day War with it Arab neighbors was the British-designed and -built Centurion tank armed with a 105mm main gun. *Robert Manasherob*

On display at the Israeli Army Tank Museum is an American-designed and -built M48 Patton medium tank in Israeli Army markings and armed with its original 90mm main gun, but powered by a diesel engine. *Robert Manasherob*

The next big step in upgrading the American-designed and -built M48 Patton medium tanks in Israeli Army service was the fitting of a British-designed 105mm main gun as seen in this picture. *Israeli Army*

The United States supplied the Israeli Army a large number of American-designed and -built M60 main battle tanks during the 1973 Yom Kipper War to make up for their combat losses. *Israeli Army*

MERKAVA III MAIN BATTLE TANK

Length:	24 feet 11 inches
Width:	8 feet 8 inches
Height:	12 feet 1.5 inches
Approximate Weight:	68 tons
Crew:	4
Armament:	120mm cannon and three machine guns

After having spent decades gaining experience on modifying the tanks of other nations, the Israeli Army decided in the early 1970s to build a brand-new tank named the Merkava, which entered service in 1977. *Robert Manasherob*

(opposite page, top) To keep its American M60A1 main battle tanks up to date, the Israeli Army has continuously improved the vehicle's armor protection levels. The newest version seen here has extra armor added to both turret and hull. *Robert Manasherob*

(opposite page, bottom) The Israeli Army has upgraded a number of captured Russian-designed T-54/55 tanks by replacing their original 100mm main gun with a 105mm British-designed main gun, as seen in this picture. *Robert Manasherob*